Judas Iscariot and other Poems

Knut Ødegård

Waxwing Books

Brian McNeil was born in Scotland in 1952. He studied Classics and Theology at the University of Cambridge (Bachelor of Arts 1973; Diploma in Theology 1974; Doctor of Philosophy 1978). He then worked as Assistant in the Faculty of Catholic Theology at the University of Vienna from March 1979 to September 1980. After a year spent studying in Oslo, he entered a monastery in Italy in October 1981 and was ordained priest in Rome in May 1985. He has worked in Munich from 1995. He speaks Norwegian fluently and has translated many books from that language into English, including "Missa", by Knut Ødegård, Dedalus Press, Dublin (2002).

Knut Ødegård

•

Judas Iscariot
and other Poems

•

Translated from Norwegian by
Brian McNeil

•

Waxwing Poems

Waxwing Poems ~ 24 The Heath ~ Cypress Downs ~ Dublin 6W
Ireland
Editor: John F. Deane

www.waxwingpoems.com

© J.W.Cappelen Publisher, Oslo; Knut Ødegård, Brian McNeil and Waxwing Poems, 2005

This translation has been published with the financial support of NORLA Non-fiction.

•
ISBN 0 9549771 0 6

Waxwing Poems are distributed in U.S.A. and Canada by
Dufour Editions Inc., P.O.Box 7, Chester Springs, Pennsylvania 19425;
in the U.K. by Central Books, 99 Wallis Rd., London E9 5LN

Waxwing Poems receives financial assistance from
An Chomhairle Ealaíon, The Arts Council, Ireland.

Printed in Dublin by Johnswood Press.

Note on the first publication of these poems.

"The Farmer" ("Bonde"): *Stephensen-huset,* Oslo 2003, 76ff.
"The Boys' Orchestra" ("Gutemusikken"): *Buktale,* Oslo 1994, 41ff.
"Drunkards and Crazy Folk" ("Drankarar og galningar"): *Biesurr, laksesprang,* Oslo 1983, 12ff.
"We moved the Beehives out There" ("Vi vandra bikubane ut dit"): *Stephensen-huset,* 37ff.
"Succession" ("Suksesjon"): *Buktale,* 69ff.
"All This" ("Alt dette"): *Kinomaskinist,* Oslo 1991, 59f.
"Window, Wide Open" ("Vindu, vidt ope"): *Buktale,* 39f.
"Priest" ("Prest"), unpublished in Norwegian
"Hilltop Farm" ("Kringsjå"), *Stephensen-huset,* 9ff.
"Signals" ("Signal"), *Kinomaskinist,* 32f.

"Judas Iscariot" ("Judas Iskariot"): *Stephensen-huset,* 81ff.

Contents

The Farmer	9
The Boys' Orchestra	13
Drunkards and Crazy Folk	17
We Moved the Beehives Out There	21
Succession	25
All This	29
Window, Wide Open	31
Priest	34
Hilltop Farm	36
Signals	45
Judas Iscariot	47

THE FARMER
Boris Magdenovski in memoriam

His hearing isn't what it was.
He is taking a dog for a walk.
He looks at the fields – the Sunday is a bright blue.
As he walks, he thinks about improvements – a new invention.
A little while ago, he was thinking about the animals' birthing,
now he is thinking about an invention.
He has a paper bag in his left hand,
his trusty stick swings in his right:

the stick swings, a glittering wheel in the blue Sunday!
Boris the farmer enjoys his walk in the village of Brezno.

The dog's hearing isn't what it was, either.
Red blood flows in the veins of man and dog.
Now Boris is thinking that things furthest off are clearest –
from here, he can see his wife Katarina who lies under tussock and cross:
the young girl's eyes see him, they darken as Boris

glides into her.
From here, he can see his grandchild Tihomir in distant Skopje
as he plays in the backyard in Partenija Sografski, Tihomir
skips over a rope.

He swings his trusty stick! Like a propeller in the Sunday blue.
The dog is snuffling along the cart-track.
The paper bag rustles a little in his left hand.
It is as if they were taking off, rushing upwards in the blue air:
a farmer, a brown dog, a paper bag with bread and yellow cheese, a cart-track
leading to the cemetery.
Up there in the air, he is thinking about his invention: a paddle wheel!
A paddle wheel in the brook for the threshing,
easy to replace with windmill sails – like wings on the barn wall –
when the brook ran dry.
Yes, we have to save electricity nowadays, thinks the farmer.
A wheel and wings – perfect!

They both hear a whistling in the air.
We don't know what the dog thinks
about the whistling. He keeps on trotting,
while the farmer's thoughts spring from rotary blades and wheel to Tihomir:

there is a whistling in the air
when the skipping rope flies between heaven and earth
in the backyard in Partenija Sografski, he thinks.
He smiles at Tihomir
and smiles at her who has been lying under tussock and cross
since nineteen ninety-two.
He is getting close now.

They see a shadow fall from the sky, gliding
down the ridge of the hill.
We don't know what the dog thinks
about the shadow. Boris the farmer thinks
of big birds' wings, and he thinks of himself as a boy
when he sprang down from the barn roof with wings of cowhide
stretched over wooden laths, wings
he had made without permission:
he glided up towards the sky
just for one second, then crashed into the cornfield. He can still feel the graze
and taste the blood when he licked his fists.

A whistling in the air, a black shadow: they walk on
in their dreams towards the cemetery

carrying a paper bag.

They don't turn round. They are on their way to Katarina.
They don't see that the shadows gliding down the hillside
aren't crows, nor geese, but men in black shirts.
This is July the first, two thousand and one, in the village of Brezno, a blue Sunday.
They don't hear the men shouting that everyone in the village
is to kneel down before the Commandant who has led them over the mountains
from Kosovo. They don't hear.
They don't see the Commandant hit thirteen-year-old Biljana on the mouth:
her mouth bleeds. Later, it is her crotch that bleeds.

They don't hear the shot fired at Boris the farmer,
his bent back that swayed so lightly
while his stick traced a glittering wheel in the air.
Boris falls.
Boris is dead.
The dog snuffles at Boris – dead.
The paper bag rustles in the scarcely perceptible wind along the cart-track.

THE BOYS' ORCHESTRA

The bass tuba's mother-of-pearl shimmering
against the soft fingers

valves, resilience, light pressure, air-
lessness? none at all: a stream
from his bird's-breast
through tight lips, into

the secret openings of the valves (shu
t/open) through the curved
and golden metal, out

in the shameful triumph of the wide outstretched funnel
over all the thirteen-year-old boys' defeats, a sousaphone!
like a tremendous unfolding of a forbidden
blossom that thrusts its bell out
of a frail boy's body, its
brass around the body against both childhood
and manhood: six-eight rhythm! The boys' music comes

with pimples and longings in a Sousa march
directed by shoemaker Kleppen
in a war on behalf of puberty's right to the streets
in all directions! The bass tuba player blows

his indifference to all defeats in clammy boys' rooms before sleep and all girls'
mocking giggles at playtime and the penniless afternoons
at the shooting gallery in the funfair,
he marches now, on the sheet-music here
with fingers dancing over the mother-of-pearl, so
soft against the mother-of-pearl shimmering, so tight
the lips against the mouthpiece. So wind-blue the sailor's cap

over the red
hair, so steel-blue the jacket over the thin
hairless bird's-breast, so blue like the sky
the trousers with straps
over his shameful snail of a cock, in a rhythm
where freckles and pimples are drowned out
by the bass tuba's imperious ore and where I myself

the smallest piccolo in the orchestra, am eternally

held fast in this rhythm which drums us onward
through the tuba's darkness and the piccolo's trills
of light.

A rhythm which still sits in the feet of middle-aged men
and makes every step we take
a steady tread in shoemaker Kleppen's footprints
over all borders – even the last. Even
the last. It holds no fears for us

old boy-musicians. We still recognise each other
after all those years. The engineer thirty years at sea
whom I met the day before yesterday in the bar, the headmaster whose
photograph they put in the paper, the man who sells packets for making wine
and insecticides, the goldsmith with the magnifying glass in his eye. The names
are gone, but that isn't so important: we
still recognise each other
by means of the mouths and fingers on invisible instruments
in bars, in newspaper photos, behind shop windows.
There is a Sousa march that lies over us. We may perhaps get old. Until we sprout

wings. But then we will get the glorified

bodies we dreamed about, and we'll get our old instruments back:
the snare drum
the clarinet an eternal afterbeat on the althorn trumpet and B-cornet and then
I myself with the piccolo up there, you know. And a tremendous sousaphone
sings through the heavenly spheres! We march
in our wind-blue uniforms up and down with our feet
on the firmament between earth and heaven and our stars and suns
of gleaming polished brass and clarinets glittering like lightning towards earth.
No, we have nothing to fear with shoemaker Kleppen at the head
of a rhythm that holds our longings fast and lifts us
through darkness and light and sun and moon and blows us through all
the starry circle of the zodiac! Stars and Stripes
forever. Trrram-tam-tam trrram-tam-tam
trrram-ta-ta ram-ta-ta tam.

Drunkards and Crazy Folk

The drunkards, with splendid names
such as Konrad or Adolf, gathered together
on the outskirts of Molde town. Sometimes their singing
was borne on the wind to us: old hits
or sad low-church hymns about the cross
and the bleeding wounds in Jesus' side. The crazy folk too
wandered around on the outskirts – people like Lundli, who had
once got his intermediary-school diploma: at night, he hewed
and sawed heavy trees, the sound cut its way into the sleep
of us children and got mixed up with dreams
about flying over the housetops or drawing up big fish
from pools with infinite darkening depths.

One day, his cross finished, Lundli went
slowly at evening in his white sheet along the High Street
with the huge cross slung over his back.
After him followed the drunkards, Konrad, Adolf
and the rest, and then a throng of children: I kept
my fingers tight around the chestnut from the cemetery tree in my pocket.

Lundli called out in his light tenor and falsetto YOU MUST TAKE
UP YOUR CROSS AND FOLLOW ME SAYS THE LORD! His words
flew like fire to Konrad and Adolf, and their big
drunkards' lips replied: "Follow me, says the Lord!
And Halleluiah! And Halleluiah!" Their white hands
danced like birds' wings in the air

The pentecostal procession passed the Alexandra Hotel.
In the windows of the wine bar were the pink faces of queers
and elderly divorcees: in his alcoholic stupor, gay
Jens in his checked sailor suit and tie stumbled down the steps
from the hotel and joined the procession. Old Hansen the
tinsmith, divorced for thirty years, with his heart full
of spittle from his own children, took his time, but
followed him and glided in the crumpled wedding-suit
that was too tight for him, his belly wobbling: he followed
right behind crazy Lundli, who sang FOLLOW ME
FOLLOW ME SAYS THE LORD FOR IT IS NOT THE HEALTHY
WHO NEED THE PHYSICIAN BUT THOSE WHO ARE SICK
OF SIN COME ALL YOU WHO HAVE SINNED and from the
direction of the quay came the clattering steps of skinny old Karen,
whose going price was a pail of beer and who knew

the town's trouser buttons and zips better than the cheerful
seamstresses: she emerged from the shack and the toilet on the quay
and drifted into the procession

Crazy Lundli was almost collapsing
under the enormous cross he had carved out
and assembled in the long dark nights, hammering it
firmly into place with rusty nails left by the German occupation.
From far away came deep rumbles, and lightning cut across the skies:
now the procession glided on to the town square and the clouds amassed
over the heads of the drunkards and crazy folk, children and queers
and divorcees and women of doubtful repute who cried out: "Halleluiah!
Praise the Lord!" as the first raindrops
squirted on to Lundli's bald pate. The vicar made an appearance
in his black robes, and the police in full uniform
and nurses in white took care of Lundli: they jabbed
syringes into him as he cried through the rain and the wind
PRAISE THE LORD ALL SINNERS FOR HIS GRACE UPON GRACE
TAKE UP THE CROSS AND FOLLOW THE LORD. Then he turned white
and fainted in the ambulance while Konrad and Adolf
held the cross firmly upright in the rainstorm in Molde town

The vicar in his black gown got up
on Lundli's margarine crate on the town square: "Go home!"
he commanded, "this is delusion, sickness, indeed
minds gone mad. Jesus did not mean it literally
when he talked about crosses, it was symbolic and
referred to 'burdens' as a theoretical concept," cried the priest
from the crazy man's crate. Then the heavens burst open
above Molde town and lightning cut a path through the darkness
like a blazing arrow towards the church tower: the bells began
to ring torrential peals, indeed the earth trembled and now the
rain was coming down like Noah's floodwater. I squelched home
in big boots, taking the shortcut across the cemetery,
snatching up the chestnuts which flowed in their green shells
from grave to grave

and after slices of bread with margarine and syrup
came the night with its dreams to us children
and to crazy folk and sinners: we flew without wings
over the town, mounting steeply like a flock of birds
with crazy Lundli and his cross at our head, rising
up to a heaven where big fish squirmed up
from bottomless depths of darkness

WE MOVED THE BEEHIVES OUT THERE

The heather bloomed best out by the windy beaches to the west.
We moved the beehives out there by the sea after the flowering season
of the pink clover in the inner arms of the fjord:
we came with the red-lacquered Ford
with room for six hives back in the luggage compartment.
It was essential to find shelter against this wind
that never lets up here.

When I was a child with Father in the eight-cylinder Ford
I thought like a child that there were foxes under the birch roots, as in the song,
while we came driving slowly westward along the gravel roads in the evenings
after the worker bees had returned to their hives,
their hind-feet heavy with nectar and pollen.

When it rained, we could start earlier, then the bees crept
around indoors with their glittering wings and devoted themselves to feeding the
larvae and transforming nectar into honey in the wax cells. Thousands of them – perhaps as many
as fifty thousand crawled around in each hive
in the rear of the car where Father and I drove.

As the car rolled slowly along the rain-grey fjord,
I thought that it would have been a fine thing to know Bjørnstjerne Bjørnson.
Father too said he must have been
a fine man, but he was dead now. I looked for foxes
but it was difficult to see the roots under the birch trunks
from the car window, they rushed past and the further out to sea we came,
the thinner were the trunks and cow-parsley grew high by the roadside
and metre-high foxgloves with nodding purple bells
before we came out on to the heather field.

It was one of the thundery summers when I thought this in the Ford. Lightning
tore across the sky, but we hummed in the downpour that followed – mostly
Bjørnson. Father drove
and I sat with the smoker and puffed little clouds of smoke into the back of the car
at bees that crept through mostly invisible slits.
When we braked by some cliffs out where the heather grew
we had to be careful not to slip on roots and mud and wet stones
as we carried the buzzing beehives out from the Ford's baggage compartment
and up the path to a spot where they could stand secure and sheltered from the sea wind.

I recognised the wild scent of wax and honey in my nostrils
as I carried the hive close in to my scrawny chest and neck, I felt

the bees crawling around inside the walls of the hive.
The song about the fox under the birch root kept on humming within me
in the cloudburst that now came after a flash of lightning
that rent the Atlantic in two like in the Bible and a bellowing like an ox rose up
from the depths of the sea and went out over the coast where Father and I stood
at the outermost rim with a beehive between us.

We stood like this: Father, and I, joined together with fifty thousand bees
crawling around in the hive we held, while sky and earth broke up around us.
But we stood in our boots, and when the storm moved away inland
towards Trollheimen, Hallingskarvet and the Swedish border,
we put down the hive in the heather field
and went down to the car and brought up the others.
We had a good rhythm in our feet now, and it occurred to me that Bjørnstjerne Bjørnson too
had been a boy here and had thought of foxes under birch roots
further in along the fjord.

We donned our beekeepers' hats with veils that fell down
across our shoulders and pulled tight all the zips in the trousers
and jackets in our white beekeepers' suits
so that we could have been in an American film about beings from outer space
landing on the earth, a big being and a little one. My job was

to handle the smoker: I broke up little pieces of compressed wood
and put them in the smoker, kindled them with a match
so that lots of smoke welled up before Father removed the boards
that shut the entrances to the hives and the bees streamed out:
to begin with, they hovered like clouds in the sky above the hives

then suddenly one group of bees veered off across the heather fields
while the others settled on the hives
or crawled around on our beekeepers' suits. We stood quite still: Father
and I, out there on the shore by the ocean that August evening,
and saw the bees return like shining arrows under the rainbow
that stretched out hugely over us.

We saw them descend, each to its hive, and stay there unmoving
with wings like wheels in the wind
only a few centimetres above the hive roofs, they stood like that a few seconds
before they started to dance in great circles over the hives
and then slowly took off in the same dance out towards the honey-wet heather
with the bee swarm following, in a mighty rushing sound that filled the heavens.

Succession

I

The different colours of piss.
The deep yellow
with its smell like honey
reminds me of autumn
at home, Father
and the process of extracting the heather-honey
when the sun screws slowly downward from
the autumn sky, glowing
behind his bent back: the hill
conceals a sun and the smell of honey
spreads across Father's country.
The water-white piss
after some days
in the hospital, like in
skim-milk, mother's
byre, there were steaming muzzles
and teats then, I drank fresh-sieved milk
out of my wooden ladle. A blue-white child, yellow

hair. A thin clergyman comes
and offers me pastoral care in this
bed in a room like this, but I
do not believe in the limited sacraments
he administers, he leaves
embarrassed by the smell of honey
and fresh-sieved milk. He lacks the apostolic
succession, the scrawny one. And perhaps I am
too much preoccupied by visible
signs of Christ's presence: I
believe.

II

I am not one of
those who deny, their Wittenberg circle
of theses, I lie
in these smells and believe. I do not deny
the seven sacraments, I do not deny
my mother and my father. I believe
in the blessed milk and honey,
and that I will come home at the last.

Sit down on the toilet
just after my old mother
had sat there. The black
ebony seat with the tepidity
of her old warmth, a little
squirt of urine, yellow like a glowing
sun that has slowly bored its way into the black
hill at home. I
believe.

III

I do not deny.
Behold, your mother, I say
to the clergyman (Lutheran): the bird-
woman in room number two
who daren't lock the loo. She
who sits like a ball of yarn on the toilet seat
when someone opens unexpectedly.
She bears all our contempt
on her wings, pastor. Laughter.
You are her son, show her

filial pastoral care, the sacraments.

Come, sweet night, vicar. Old excrement
clings to the inner walls of the toilet
bowl. It is not washed away
completely in the mornings. There is always

a remnant, vicar,
of brown in the white
porcelain. The old bird-woman
who is your mother has pressed
with unlocked door through the night
a grey turd, and the one who had the gall-bladder operation
his dark-brown shit
with specks in it. Come, sweet night, vicar,
there is always a remnant
left over.

ALL THIS
    (for Þorgerður)

When we grow old, my dear,
and the crows come to get us
(caw-caw, then off with one beat of their wings, into the air),
where will our love be then?

Where will this mouth be then that says
something about a broken coffee-machine, rust on the car, a visit to the
cardiologist, a filling that has fallen out, the phone bill
or (romantic) about the golden moon
and the rowan-tree in blossom, which explains away all the white
lies, the cheatings, and all it doesn't manage to say about the child
we never had, and that melts together with yours in a kiss?

Or these eyes that stare into the green computer screen day
out and day in and that look at you when you take your clothes off as evening draws on:
you put the light out modestly and stand like a silhouette with ripe breasts
and thighs against the light that seeps thinly
in through the windows from the cobalt-blue Iceland Sea?
Or these hands that write and write, that put

the snow-shovels in their place and caress you
over your limbs until you burn and want to have me
like a force that smashes into the dams, and I explode
cascading into you, into your womb that was removed by a surgeon
in Reykjavik?

All this that we call love –
where will it be, when the crows come?
For they will not take us both together. One of us
will be the first to lie out there on the ground dirtied by snow
down by the sea (yellow last year's grass, churned-up spring snow)
when the black crows come and pick at the mouth,
the eyes, the hands, the genitals.

That one of us who is left behind the window then, dear,
who wakes in the mornings and does everything
we are familiar with – fetches in *Morgunblaðið* which sits
in the letterbox. Turns on the taps
and looks at oneself in the mirror: Does that one of us then see something more
than one's own face there? Will the other face then
shine through the face in the mirror, as abandoned houses
stand and shine by the sea?

WINDOW, WIDE OPEN

As when a virus
leaves the body,

suddenly
gone, under the lid of dark septic tanks. The pipes roar
in the municipal waterworks, someone is opening taps

or out of a window, towards clouds
and faces

and all this I feel as if for the first time
after a strong fever has loosened its grip on my eyes
and ears. Your face, darling: a window
that has suddenly swung open! A childhood
in rustling grass by the white house

and you open your window
to meet my manhood which lustfully
enters in where childhood youth and age

are all equally and dizzyingly close.

Your window
towards scurrying white clouds. Wide open! Behind it
our faces are timelessly naked. Our love
is here, and it is only time
that passes. We no longer need to
explain ourselves to each other, darling! Our faces
explain us: there is no death, no
ageing. Love is stronger than death,

I daren't say, afraid of making a fool of myself, should have said:
Do you remember? Was that Jesus' words or the vicar's words,
uttered in the little church all those years ago? It was in August. You
stood there with white lilies, yourself a white
lily: a bride in August. Stronger
than death! And you caress me now, as if you know my thoughts,

stroking my bald pate with such infinite tenderness, as if I were (despite everything)
exempt from all the decay time brings, all the sin, and I swim
like a finely polished cranium through soil, a seed
making towards a great resurrection in love.

Under the white scurrying clouds. In towards you. Up into you

rises my love out of this virus which is time and forgetfulness.
You swing your window wide open: there is
no death! Everything is
as if for the first time, darling. Grass
grows around my childhood house, there is a roaring
in the pipes in the municipal waterworks, somebody opens
and opens taps.

Priest

Uncle Knut was a priest.
He was a practical man, but Latin
was Greek to him.
He died after his retirement, he stood
and dug the site for the new house
when his heart gave way.

He was more an electrician
than a preacher, he began all his speeches
by saying: "I'm not much of a one for speeches"
and he was right about that.

He did not really have much to teach
his parishioners, they had their own troubles
with their births, with their love and their death
and he did not have words for such things.

But he had learnt how to repair
electric wires and he visited people in their homes
and mended short circuits and defective
fuse boxes, he screwed lamps into place

and wherever he had been, there was light.

Hilltop Farm

"Hilltop" is the name of a little farm, as far up as you can get skywards
above Molde town, outside the world.
Great-grandfather Knut broke open the soil here, his life was the scythe
which flew in summer in the haymaking season, and godly books in winter
under the Plough which rolled just above his shiny pate, as well as some
cows and sheep, and hens that jumped around.

I thought of old Knut when I went with the sun on my back
today and followed my own shadow, it stretched
so long in December's country, outside the world
and up in the hillsides the shadow stretched, almost right up to the top.
Soon we will be the same age, I thought, as I went
and remembered his daughter, my grandmother in her wicker chair
on the glassed-in veranda who said that it rained corn
over her father, golden. She rattled her knitting needles,
probably she meant: he sowed and harvested.

Well, what do I know, where I swing my stick, holding
the carved eagle's head with a light grip and following my own shadow?
I see a man climbing up on to the church roof
to repair the bronze bells that have been jammed in Molde for a long time now.
YOU ARE HERE. WE'RE COMING SOON
says the sign on the bus stop. Here?

I am walking in my childhood. Older people
often do that. That's how I will be soon, just as old as
grandmother Kristine in the glassed-in veranda and great-grandfather Knut at Hilltop Farm,
right up skywards somewhere.
The circular bus comes. Soon I will be old enough
to get a children's ticket, and soon
the bus will not stop at the last stop on the hillside,
but will drive up as far as you can get, will follow the endless shadow
right up to the stars above Hilltop Farm where I get off the bus
and board the shining Plough, feel dizzy
like an infant in a pram with mighty springs and wheels
through the heavens.

*

But stop! I forgot that we were musical
up on the hillside, and a little superior there
under the sky's broad roof. Now I see in the register
that great-grandfather's Hilltop Farm had only a small taxable value (0,94) when he bought
the soil he had wrestled with for fifty years, in 1908 he
and my clairvoyant great-grandmother Serianna from Hoem became the owners
of a piece of land right outside polite society, so steep
that ordinary people in the town lost their footing and tumbled down in the streets.
She smoked a pipe
and read Norway's future in the coffee dregs while Knut
broke open the soil and mowed the steep slope with his short scythe and
wrote in the Bible with his clumsy fingers
the name of every child "born to the world"
up there under the sky,
sat on a straight-backed chair and wrote
with his back to an oleograph of Jesus and the disciples.
I sit with that Bible beside me now.

People say I have grandmother Kristine's face.
She and the other deceased hang
on the walls here.
Knut and Serianna in a little metal frame: the emulsion

is gradually cracking in the thin photographic paper
glued on to stiff card, flakes
of their faces and hands are falling off and white threads
and spots are spreading on their black Sunday-best,
the silver.
I see in the bathroom mirror that I have traits
of both of them.
On my way down to the town I glimpse my face in the storefront glass
of the supermarket together with tins of ham and posters, there I see
grandmother Kristine.
When I come down to the High Street I get a glimpse of myself
reflected in the huge window of the County Bank that looks on to the square:
there I see
great-grandfather Knut, soon my pate will be as bald as his
on the photographic paper, while I cross the square
I look briefly at the spring fashions
and I see my happy mother, died in '99 (but before Alzheimer's
and all that), reflected among miniskirts
and lace underwear on plastic models wearing makeup:
My happy mother on the hillside! Whose grandmother Serianna taught her
to read the future in dregs
and who sat on old Knut's knee

and pulled at his beard, and who gave birth to me who am walking and looking
at the reflections in the window panes here. Who take my place in the circular bus:
an elderly man with many faces, as if
the dead were reflecting themselves in mirror upon mirror in me: the bus goes
upwards now, up swings and steep slopes, higher up
and lets people off. I am left sitting alone
and this bus does not stop before it gets right up there
at Hilltop Farm.
Now there is aurora borealis, it resembles grandmother's green silk dress
which rolls slowly over the sky.

Old people have crazy thoughts, everyone knows that.
I thought that if I turned round, up here,
I would see my face reflected in the Atlantic Ocean
or the Indian Ocean or the Pacific:
in a little mirror in the planet Tellus which revolves
slowly around itself down there, but – as in a glimpse –
allows me to see my own face here from above the aurora borealis: thus.

*

Small spruce-trees with fluttering petticoats

I saw them through the bus window, and I thought of
my sisters. They too don't
come here any more.

This bus is not driving back. We practised
each in turn, it was Chopin's deep bass notes
that were my problem. My left pinkie

all the way down on the piano in Mazurka op. 7, nr. 1. *Vivace,* lively
3/4 beat: the treble clef directs the right thumb
towards a quaver F, semi-quaver pause, semi-quaver F, crotchet
G and crotchet A, but the bass clef drives the left pinkie
towards a crotchet F down there in the piano's cellar and up with the pinkie,
index finger, thumb to a crotchet F, C, E flat in the octave above
in a rhythmic grasp by three doughy fingers: plung pling-pling.
Those soft white fingers of mine!
They couldn't manage the third bar in Chopin's Mazurka … from the second
beat with the crescendo into forte fortissimo in the third bar, and there:
the left pinkie and thumb fluttered to grasp
a whole octave from E to E in a mighty crotchet beat

at the piano teacher's, colonel's wife
with an eagle's nose: swissssh
from her ruler which smacks the white
pinkie that landed on F and lay like a snail
on her beautiful piano under the painting
of the colonel who won the war against the Germans. Swisssh,
so wordless my finger is lost.

Small spruce-trees with fluttering petticoats.
My sisters then, and I was a little larch-tree
in short trousers, when Mother's shining lacquered Rönich piano
(bought for the money she got from selling eggs) came on a lorry
jolting up the gravel road towards the hillside, blue smoke
skywards: it opened its wings
in the farmyard. Grandmother Kristine was eaten up by cancer
at that time, but grandfather Hol and Father unscrewed the doors of the house
and carried the piano in.
I can still hear the piano strings play
all by themselves when they carried it in.

Small spruce-trees. The bus swings
and I think of my sisters

and of the resin that flows out of the openings and scratches in the spruce-tree:
thick, sticky discharge of resin in turpentine, rank yellow smell
on my fingers.
No, the bus is not turning back.
I raise my left hand and sniff the stiff
pinkie: I can still smell a faint odour of resin.

The sisters who play and play the piano in this musical
hillside here. In their fluttering petticoats. But Father was silent,
he took me hunting. Out on the moors we went,
outside Hilltop Farm.
Mostly dead rabbits and carcasses of grouse that dangled under the dark
cellar roof, bloodstains on the floor.

But there is a music up there, I hear it
here from down in the cellar. There is a Chopin
up there, right up on Hilltop Farm. He sounds more clearly
in my ears now, with their weakened sense of hearing, when the bus ascends.

*

Ah yes, there is a yellow (faded) book of exercises

from the 1940's: Schirmer's Library
of Musical Classics, piano solo collections,
with neat writing in pencil: Fingerings! With feeling! But it is first of all Mother
I think of now, I think of Mother who calls
into the moors at evening
to him I call blood daddy
and to me, so

there are no more shadows, December's
sun casts its short rays on the soil here by us.

Mother who calls into the moors in me
now, white hoarfrost. She stands with the blue veins
and holds a piece of knitting by a thread

which disappears in an endless ball of yarn in there

behind Mother, where she stands framed
as in a wide-open door

through the bus window skywards and calls
to me

SIGNALS

The moon is a wheel

Owl-eyes wheels
within wheels

The rainbow through heaven
and earth: the circular communion rail, the heavens
seven fold themselves into wheels. A spring
wound up in a tremendous clockwork: time-
machines, priestly ships
right through the universe, fire-chariots

I sleep in my dizzying
bed in Molde, while Tellus
turns round
and round. The moon round as a ball
in owl-eyes, owl-eyes
in the tree that scrapes against the thin wall

There is someone who says: God!
on Earth, as she circles and spins. There are
dreams about dog teams down there, who hunt
across atlases, maps and globes
to reach the last white spaces

And there are weak signals
endlessly far away, all the way from within
your heart, almost only as interference
in the finely tuned listening devices in the observation posts
which fold themselves out like wheels
towards the universe, which say: Yes, my child.

JUDAS ISCARIOT

1.

He came from an out of the way place in Judea, Kerioth,
where a waterhole like a weeping eye in the blowing
sand maintained life in a few farmers with creaking
ass-drawn carts. Prophetic words sent forth

from a house of prayer patiently built up of sand and glue to resist the black wind
that sometimes came and settled, choking, over Kerioth
like the fluttering wings of huge dying birds from the Dead Sea –
but sometimes the wind held its breath, and the eye in the waterhole
saw the heavenly constellations flowing clearly in the black sea over its head

at night. Then the village comes to life in the morning, the sun
warms even the dead in the village cemetery, and young women
emerge from the sand-blown houses, their breasts heavy with milk,
and draw water from the well. They wash and anoint Kerioth's youngest
Jewish villagers in the good breeze. Then the wind starts up again

and prophetic words rise up to meet this wind which is older
than the world and comes from nowhere and leads to
nowhere and these grains of sand that are more numerous than the stars
when the Lord permits us to count them, more numerous than all the plagues
the Lord's chosen people must endure: grasshoppers and scorpions
in our endless wanderings through the wilderness, and Rome's legions of unbelievers

and the landscape begins to flicker in the burning desert wind
over Kerioth.

He was of the house of David, and hence a distant
relative of the one they later called Messiah.

It came to pass in those days that a decree went forth
from the emperor Augustus that all the world should be enrolled
in a census, and all walked or rode or came in their carts
to be enrolled, each to his own town.
Simon went up from Kerioth to the city of David
which is called Bethlehem, together with Judith his wife
who was pregnant, and with her daughter whom she had
with a foreign soldier who had come with the wind.

But it came to pass while they were there, that the time came
for her to give birth.
And she gave birth to her son, the first-born, and wrapped him
and laid him in a manger, since there was no room for them
in the inn.

There were some shepherds out in the fields
keeping watch over their flocks by night. They said that an angel
had stood before them and the glory of the Lord had shone
around them, and they were terrified.
And the angel said: "Be not afraid!
For I proclaim to you a great joy
which will be for all the people.
Today a saviour is born for you, who is Christ the Lord,
in the city of David."

And Judith saw the shepherds come into the stable
but they stopped at another manger: she noted the names
Joseph and Mary from Nazareth while she held her newborn first son
up against the shepherds' dark backs.

That was how Judas looked into Jesus' eyes for the first time

with an infant's unclear glance, unfocused,
like one who gazes down into a well.

2.

They nailed Him fast.
Soon I will be dangling loose
in the air: I'll get a
bluish-violet head, my eyes will bulge,
my tongue will become a serpent
that darts out in the desert sand
and the blue erect penis will spurt out
its white seed in this wind's
gaping empty thighs.
But He was the one who betrayed.

There is a yellow wind
that never stops in me: His betrayal
was mine.
This isn't how I meant it to be.

3.

They laughed at me because I was weaned so late.
When my two younger siblings came, Mother always had a little over for me
in her breasts. She loved me more than the others.
With her sweet milk on my tongue I held my lips
tight closed when I went out into the eternal wind.
No one was better at school than I was. I tie the knot in the rope
and think of Mother: I was to have brought honour to the family.
I compensated for my shameful sister, whom Mother bore to our enemy,
by my hard work at school.
I don't remember Father's skin any more: I think of sand
and salt and parchment and brown sweat.
He welcomed Mother and my shameful sister into
his priestly family.
He was well thought of as a preacher among the sheep-farmers
in Kerioth and the surrounding villages.

I was head and shoulders taller than the others.
They had to look up to me.
I was a child with lovely curls, who read
history books: they were my joy

and my raging, and I wanted to save this country.
I knew the songs by heart. They are singing
in me now, as I interweave three strands:
I am weaving the rope.
The teachers loved me more than the others: no one
was more zealous in preparing for the coming of the Messiah
with justice for our crushed people.
They had to look up to me.
I knew that they laughed at me because of my weak chin.

4.

When I saw Him, I recognized Him,
as if I had seen Him before: I thought
He was the one who was to come. His betrayal
was mine.
This isn't how I meant it to be.

They said that His mother too
was a woman with a past. They whispered
that Joseph was not His father.
Then I felt an even stronger bond between us.

I was tall and thin as a youngster.
My voice was high when I sang and strummed the strings: like myrrh
like balsam sweet as honey and milk, said Mother.
It is night. I sit in the potter's field, a black ring
around the white full moon. The strands wriggle
like serpents in my hand.

I let my beard grow down from my underlip
towards my neck when I saw Him three years ago.
There were hundreds of us flocking around Him, we recognized
the spirit's wind when He spoke to us.
When He chose his twelve, I was one of them.
We set out two by two, we went in six directions and proclaimed
that the time was close at hand.

The yellow wind doesn't trouble me so much now.
Here I sit in this field among earthworms and maggots,
the wind has crept into my body.
But when He whispered confidentially with the beardless
John and leant back against the chatterbox Peter
I felt the sulphurous wind seep
in through my nostrils.

I was not a doubter. When the masses turned
against us, I was not one of those who went away.
When I came home to Kerioth and preached,
the teachers said that He was an enemy of Judah.
I shook the dust of my home town from off my feet.

I gave up Mother and Father and my teachers for Him.
Now he was my all.

He had such strange eyes, I had seen them before
as in a cloudy mirror or well: I glimpsed a tremendous burst of starlight,
a celestial song down there in the depths.
He gave me the purse, I looked after the money.
The worst thing was leaving Mother.

5.

And it was night.
He went out quickly, but no matter where he turned
it seemed he was turning his back
on the constellations above the city: all he saw was his own
endless shadow slithering like a dark tongue over obscure outlines

of paths and houses and out into the dark air.
Then his dog growled softly and the morning cock
crowed in the potter's house.

He knew that Pisces was the sign of Judea
and Saturn Israel's star, he was
a learned man here on earth. He did not see
clearly now, not the sign of Pisces, for the leaves
were rustling and the yellow wind stung
in his eyes, he grasped the rope
his dog was dragging after him, it tightened
around the animal's neck
and the animal found its way over the cobblestones.

His errand was to prevent this betrayal.

6.

I had the purse, a sign of great trust. I saved money
to give strength to the crushed.
They said I took some of the money, but that is not true.
I put a little aside until the time was ripe,

and when His madness erupted, it was necessary.

They said He worked miracles.
I didn't see Him walk on the water, and what is the point
of tricks?
He was not the only one to heal the sick, but He did
have warm hands, I am a fair man.

They said He raised up the dead Lazarus.
I was not there, but I heard he was sick.
And what good is that supposed to do?
The people might believe He was a heavenly being –
they might begin to speak in tongues, and the legionaries would stream in
over the land in their thousands to put an end to the madness.

But I knew I was born to share life
with this man, as if we had been foster-brothers
from the time we were held at the breast and sucked the sweet milk
dripping down on us from a young mother's breast
under the mighty stars that shone over holy Judea, I thought:
I will sacrifice everything for love of Him.
I knew I was chosen.

Call it madness, even sickness if you like,
what happened to Him after He'd begun with such manly vigour
to blow new life into our people who had grown so sluggish.

I was there when He overturned the tables of the merchants
in the temple and swung the rope over them.
I was there when He cried out: "Do not think
I have come with peace, I have come with a sword!"

There were women who clung to Him.
There was that Mary Magdalene: "What
are we to do with His madness?"
I asked.
They refused to listen. Peter placed
his huge ear, overgrown with wax, against my mouth.
John blushed in the light that shone from that face
where the madness was plain to see
for anyone with normal understanding.

I asked what all this would come to?
What would this come to, when the money
was squandered by Mary on ointments and perfume

with which she anointed His body:
she leant over Him, lightly clothed,
with swaying breasts. I turned away. Here I sit

and hear a crackling in the branches, a rustling whisper
of insects and toads as they creep around me in the field.
But the dog lies quietly at my feet. I loosen the leash
from his neck, it will make a fine noose
and I tie it to the rope with a knot: then I sling
the rough end over a black leafless branch
at which the dog's yellow eyes gaze.

7.

He was not without dreams.
Often he dreamed that he was without words.
An infant in a dark barn
abandoned. He dreamed of the smells of hay
and milk and the rank odour of dung, of horse piss
and the sounds of whinnying animals, hens cackling
and snorting pigs.
He dreamed about his mother's back, turned away,

and then his screams woke him up (in the dream)
and he looked into the eyes of another child
who lay there.
The other child laid his hands
on him, and they shared a kind of cradle-fellowship
and in the dream he kissed the other child.
When he woke, he recognized those eyes
and after such dreams he was tormented by stars
which stuck fast like sand to the inside of his eyeball.
On such days he said little, but kept close
to Him.

He had never seen angels.

8.

I was there at the feast in Lazarus' home
just before Passover. It was Mary Magdalene
who took us with her to her famous brother
in Bethany.
It was meant to be just the twelve us and Him
in the party, the women Mary and her sister Martha

were to make the meal and serve it.
But a gang of uneducated persons gathered together
outside the house to see the miracle-man and Lazarus
after he had risen from the tomb in his stinking grave-clothes.
I felt sick, I had dreamed that night,
the white grains of sand flickered in my skull.
I tried to close my eyelids again
but I felt Him move away when I laid my hand
on His robe.

We had had red wine and food, and the one
who had to all appearances been dead
slapped his fat thigh, drank more wine, and laughed
at Peter's tall tales of the blue whales he had caught
on his hook in Lake Genesareth.

Then through my sore half-opened eyes I saw
how Mary M. waved to Him to leave the table
and drew Him down on to a carpet.
She lay over Him, lay there astride him with her round backside
in the air and let down her mane of hair, which flowed
over Him: she began to rub His feet

with genuine nard-oil imported from the Himalayas,
worked her way up over His body, His thighs, rubbed
with her slender fingers and dried Him
with her own hair!

My eyes stung, my head
was like a wasps' nest, but somebody had to put a stop
to this madness and I cried out desperately
that things have reached the limit now, now things have gone far enough,
those drops are costly,
worth three hundred denarii at least: Why? Why
was not this superfluous vanity sold
and the money given to the faithful of Judah's tribe?

White wasps buzzed behind my eyes
and the room was filled to bursting
with the fragrant perfume and I was without words
and slid into a mist there, without dreams,
perhaps for a few seconds only, and I saw
that this shameful act of love did not stop
and I thought I heard Him say: Let her do it,
for she has kept this oil for my burial.

This was six days before the Passover. When I came to my senses
I had made my decision.
No one was to come between me and the great deed.
The day after, He took His seat on a ridiculous ass
and rode like a loser westward over the country fields
the three kilometers into Jerusalem.

9.

This I did for Him
I loved Him who betrayed

One who has loved is never completely alone, I have
the dog

Was there anything else?

With the noose around my neck, the rope
in the branch, I stand with my toes
on the dog. Was there anything else?

The dog twists his head round and licks my feet,

that is how he anoints me
When he gets up and goes away, there is nothing more

What I did, I did
I asked them to look after Him
They gave me thirty pieces of silver, a risible sum
I put them in the purse

They were learned men, like myself
We had read Hippocrates, we knew our Greek and Latin
He was a sick man, crazy
A disequilibrium between *sanguis, phlegma,*
chole and *melaina chole,*
a rational empirical analysis
He needed to be locked up, that is what the learned men wanted
He was not the one I had thought
but I loved Him all the same

There was no betrayal in their eyes
I was just to give them a sign to show which one He was

In the garden I kissed Him for the last time: the sign

His lips were soft like the infant in my dream,
He tasted of milk and honey

Is madness a betrayal? The dog
lies under my feet, still
Rather a case of betrayal as a result of madness
he looks at me with yellow eyes
like the full moon over the potter's field

They gave Him to Pilate
This isn't how I meant it to be

I was there, with the dog
I heard the people cry

10.

It may well be that Pontius Pilate was an upright man.
He came from one of Rome's best families, had studied
jurisprudence, philosophy and military strategy, as well as rhetoric.

Tiberius Julius Caesar appointed him procurator

over Palestine twenty-six years after the great census.
Otherwise, our sources are vague, it is like staring
down and looking for a face in a muddy well.
Josephus and Philo, Jewish authors, see a greedy man
with a hard heart.
Luke, a Greek physician and author, gives us a portrait of a weak
but fair man who wanted to let Jesus go
after an admonition and a few strokes of the scourge.
John, a Jewish-Christian author (and apostle?) makes him
a nervous intellectual who let Jesus be slapped around, scourged,
crowned him with thorns, put a purple cloak on him,
and then asked: What is truth?

Pilate disliked the Jews and the stifling heat in Jerusalem.
He had thin, white skin and lived by the sea, in Caesarea
where the cooling winds swept bluely in from the Mediterranean.
In the course of his official duties he had to sit in judgment in Jerusalem
with its narrow streets, sweat, stink and sickly heat
and stay as guest of the uneducated petty king Herod, whom he despised.
He sweats:

What is truth? – while the blood runs down the cheek

of the other man.

Judas from Kerioth in Judea, of David's stock, stood among the people
who shrieked as if they were at the stadium
and demanded that the judge release Barabbas
but kill Jesus.
The dog gazed at the one crowned with thorns, the crowd of people
pressed forward from all sides with their cry for blood
and crucifixion.
The sand behind his eyeball began to chafe when a ray of sunlight
glittered from the legionary's golden eagle and he saw everything
as if from inside a wasps' nest of golden larvae and insect wings:

Pilate's mouth
moves slowly,

like a dried-up leaf
slowly
downwards, falls into

the black darkness of a well, mud

without language, lost

The mouth slowly in the mud at the bottom of the well.
Judas read on the frog-lips:
Iesus Nazarenus Rex Iudaeorum.

11.

The sultry heat lay like a lid
over his head, Pilate could scarcely
move his mouth. At nights he lay out in the cool corridor

but even when he lay there and gazed up at the constellation
Pisces he breathed in dry sand. It seemed that all life
withered away, the blood coagulated
in the veins of the plants and crumbled into clods like sand.
Was he really dreaming, then?
He thought he heard a distant thunder from far off
but when he sat up he saw the almost half-obliterated shadow
of a man and a dog down there, disappearing in the direction of the temple.
A low growling remained there on the cobblestones, he gasped for air.

The dog stopped outside the temple, the man
let go of the leash. They stood immobile
until day dawned. Judas

hesitated a little, took hold of the leash.
The man and the dog went back to the square
where people had begun to gather.
It was Friday morning.

After the trial and the undignified presentation
Pilate lay down again in his cool corridor. The air
was even sultrier, a sour moisture trickled out
from every pore in his body. The new garment the tailor
in Rome had sent stuck to his body. Stretching out
his arm for his wineglass he heard the rumbling
of distant thunder once more
and his thoughts turned briefly to the man from Nazareth
but the wine tasted of gall and he let the glass
fall to the stone floor.

The air was utterly still now, like jelly
and he struggled to get up

when he heard the rumblings nearer at hand.
He saw the man and the dog down there still, disappearing
in at the temple gate. When the first drops

hit his tortured forehead the man
and the dog came out of the temple again, in the direction
of the potter and it was suddenly
darker. The thunder crashed now, and lightning
sliced its path over the sky: the darkness
lay thick on Jerusalem and the air like jelly
dissolved in cascading water zigzag lightning
and flood waves streaming down on the temple square.

When a mighty lightning flash hit the temple, Pilate hurried in
wet through. The peals of thunder made the solid residence
tremble, and he smiled at the thought of superstitious Herod
with his fear of angels and demons and the resurrection of the dead.

12.

For Him I loved – He who betrayed –
I betrayed

Moon sand
in my eyes, yellow
dog

that's all that's left, innocent blood
streams up towards the fishes
in the sky

The dog moves: if he goes
now

the noose will fall tight around my neck

I see unclearly the fish teem
in the constellation in the sky, as if in a
sea infinitely

deep there I sink
not
but will dangle

The dog gets up, I

glide

out in the air

now, I shall dangle
on a rope, I

will soon stink in the wind, my belly
swells out, and Judas Iscariot

bulges out in the rain and will be scorched
in the sun, those eyes
that saw Him suffer for my guilt
will be pecked out by birds, the mouth

will scream without tongue and lips
in the desert wind over Palestine

and over all the lands: His name
and over all the seven seas in the wind:

His name His name

The Waxwing Series of poetry books:

1. **"Poem"**, by Amir Or, translated from the Hebrew by Helena Berg and Fiona Sampson, with an afterword by Fiona Sampson.

2. **"Without Shoe or Horse"**, by Uilliam English, translated from the Irish by Pádraig J. Daly.

3. **"Judas Iscariot and Other Poem**s", by Knut Ødegård, translated from the Norwegian by Brian McNeil.